The
Connell Short Guide
to
Kazuo Ishiguro's

Never Let Me Go

by
David Isaacs

Contents

NOTES

Introduction

Never Let Me Go (2005) has attracted superlative after superlative. "A clear frontrunner to be the year's most extraordinary novel," began Peter Kemp's review in *The Sunday Times*. In 2010, the popular American magazine *Time* called it "the best novel of the decade". More recently, in 2015, James Wood – one of the most influential critics of his generation – has labelled it "a miraculous novel". It has sold more than a million copies worldwide and has been translated into over 40 languages.

But no-one seems to know quite what to make of it. Even its biggest admirers emphasise how strange it is. The writer Geoff Dyer, in a review for *The Independent*, calls it a "very weird book". Theo Tait agrees, writing in *The Daily Telegraph*: "*Never Let Me Go* is a very strange novel." Tait continues: "[It] is not exactly an enjoyable experience. There is no aesthetic thrill to be had... except that of a writer getting the desired dreary effect exactly right." Similarly, James Wood, despite thinking the novel "miraculous", seems puzzled by its banality, describing its prose as "excruciatingly ordinary" and stressing its "dizzying dullness [and] punitive blandness". "So bland is this voice," he writes, "so banal its daily discourses, that the reader has a kind of amazed admiration for Ishiguro's freakish courage." In his review of Ishiguro's most recent novel, *The Buried Giant*, Wood is still mystified:

"*Never Let Me Go* contained passages that appeared to have been entered into a competition called The Ten Most Boring Fictional Scenes."

So why, if it's so strange and perhaps even so boring, is *Never Let Me Go* so admired? It may well have something to do with how unexpectedly moving readers, reviewers and critics have consistently found the book. Wood writes of its "great and speculative emotional power". The Singaporese critic Wai-chew Sim puts it well, if academically, when he describes an unaccountable "existential distress" that the novel "generates" in its readers. Similarly, the critic Sarah Kerr describes "a mounting existential distress that hangs around long after we read it". Perhaps the novelist M. John Harrison captures best the strange and deep feeling the novel leaves you with, in his review for *The Guardian*:

> readers may find themselves full of an energy they don't understand and aren't quite sure how to deploy. *Never Let Me Go* makes you want to have sex, take drugs, run a marathon, dance – anything to convince yourself that you're more alive, more determined, more conscious, more dangerous than any of these characters.

A summary of the plot

Kathy H. introduces herself. Enigmatically, she tells us that she's spent the last 12 years as a "carer", looking after "donors" before they "complete". Now that her time as a carer has come to an end, she says, she wants to go over some of her memories.

In Part One, Kathy recalls her childhood in an idyllic English boarding school called Hailsham. Her memories are muddled and vague but certain things become clear. There is something unusual about this school. It has a strong emphasis on creativity: students are encouraged to create works of art, the best examples of which are taken away by a mysterious figure they call "Madame" (who sometimes hangs around the school but never speaks to them) for display in her "gallery", whose purpose is unclear. They have regular "Exchanges", where they exchange artworks and poems, and less regular "Sales", when boxes of second-hand junk are delivered to the school and the children excitedly shop for their favourite objects. They have weekly health checks, over-specific sex education lessons, and it is constantly drilled into them that it is far worse for them to smoke than it is for other teenagers. They have neither surnames nor parents. They know very little of the outside world; they know they're "special".

Most of the narration deals with Kathy's

friendship with Ruth – a bossy girl – and with Tommy – a boy with "a bad temper but a big heart" (251). Through Kathy's detailing of seemingly insignificant events, it becomes clear that she is in love with Tommy and feels inferior to Ruth. One of the longest episodes involves a cassette Kathy buys at a Sale: an old jazz album called *Songs After Dark* by Judy Bridgewater, which becomes a prized possession. Kathy is particularly taken with a song on the tape called "Never Let Me Go". She is dancing alone to it in her dorm room one day, when she becomes aware of "Madame" standing in the doorway, watching her, with tears streaming down her face. Madame walks away without saying a word; shortly afterwards, the tape disappears. Withdrawn from the outside world, the students at Hailsham have developed their own mythology, according to which Norfolk is a place in which lost things are found: the young Kathy hopes that one day she will visit Norfolk and find the tape. Ruth, meanwhile – who is now Tommy's girlfriend – buys Kathy a different tape to make up for the loss. Though she's jealous of their relationship, it's an act of kindness that touches Kathy.

As they grow older, the children learn more about who they are: they are clones, they discover, brought into the world to incubate spare organs for "normals" – ordinary citizens. When they leave school, they will become "donors": their organs will be harvested. After four "donations", they will "complete": they will die. Thanks to them, sickness has become a thing of the past.

In Part Two, Kathy remembers the time immediately after they leave Hailsham. She, Tommy and Ruth move to a kind of residential complex they call "the Cottages", where they spend a year or two trying to lead something approaching normal lives, before becoming "carers" (people who look after "donors") and, after that, "donors" themselves. They read books, explore their sexualities, go for long walks, bicker.

On a day trip to Norfolk, Tommy, recalling their childhood mythology, half-seriously suggests he and Kathy look for the tape she lost as a girl. Kathy thinks the idea ridiculous but, miraculously, they find it in a charity shop. Tommy buys it: Kathy is deeply moved by the gesture.

Also on this trip, some of their new friends tell them about a rumour they've heard: that if two Hailsham students can prove they're in love, then they will be granted a "deferral": their lives will be extended by two or three years. This, Tommy thinks, might be why Madame collected their art: to see into their souls in order to tell if a couple seeking a deferral are truly compatible. Tommy and Ruth, who are still together, think about applying for a deferral. Ruth relentlessly and cruelly taunts Kathy about her relationship with Tommy. Kathy, unable to bear it, applies to become a carer early, knowing that it will hasten her death. She leaves the Cottages and doesn't see the others for ten years.

In Part Three, Kathy turns to more recent memories. Ten years after leaving the Cottages, she's still a carer, but both Tommy and Ruth are donating: Kathy is caring for them. They broke up shortly after Kathy left and haven't seen each other since. They're both nearing "completion" and Ruth suggests that she and Kathy visit Tommy one last time. When they're all together, Ruth tells them that she always knew they were in love and that she deliberately kept them apart out of jealously. As an act of atonement, she hands them a piece of paper, on which is written Madame's address: she wants them to apply for a deferral.

After Ruth has "completed", Tommy and Kathy find "Madame" and learn that such a thing doesn't exist. "You're by yourselves," Madame tells them (267). Hailsham, she reveals, was an experiment, an attempt to give the clones – who are not popularly regarded as human – a good life before giving up their vital organs. Her gallery was an attempt to communicate their humanity to the population: not to reveal their souls, but "*to prove you had souls at all*" (255). Evidently, the public weren't convinced: Hailsham closed, and clones are now reared in farmyard conditions. Tommy, Kathy and Ruth are the lucky ones.

Tommy and Kathy try to enjoy their last few months together, but it's a struggle: Tommy asks

Kathy to stop being his carer and they part. Kathy has received the call up to become a donor. In just a few months, she will complete.

The Strange

From my summary, it might sound like *Never Let Me Go* is set in some grim, dystopian future. But it isn't. The very first thing the novel tells us is that it's an historical novel: it begins with the words: "England, late 1990s." This is our past, but a recent past, a past that many readers will have a clear memory of. The novel is emphatically grounded in the familiar.* Very quickly, however, we realise that this version of the past is, as the academic John Mullan puts it, "removed from any historical reality that we can recognise". The novel pulls in two directions: its subject matter (human cloning) gestures to our future, its setting to our past, but it's neither. This odd, futuristic history is set "not", as the novelist Margaret Attwood writes, "in

* *Never Let Me Go* is alone amongst Ishiguro's novels in this respect. His first two, *A Pale View of Hills* (1982) and *An Artist of the Floating World* (1986) are both set in post-war Japan; his third, *The Remains of the Day* (1989) is set in post-war England; his fourth, *The Unconsoled* (1995), in a surreal landscape in a generic European country; his fifth, *When We Were Orphans* (2000) in early-20th century Shanghai and London; his seventh, *The Buried Giant* (2015), in a mythological Britain of the sixth or seventh century.

Britain-yet-to-come, but in Britain-off-to-the-side".

It is a Britain in many respects identical to our own ("hideously familiar" is Attwood's phrase), but with a number of faintly discordant details woven into its fabric.* As Attwood has noticed, for example, Tommy "who is the best boy at football" is "picked on because he's no good at art... [but i]n a conventional school it would be the other way round".

Hailsham doesn't operate like conventional schools; its students don't operate like us. They have habits and customs that are slightly different to ours, described glancingly, as if they're nothing out of the ordinary. Kathy remembers, for example, how they used to listen to music:

> *several people [would] sit on the grass around a single Walkman, passing the headset around... You listened for maybe twenty seconds, took off the headset, passed it on. After a while, provided you kept the same tape going over and over, it was surprising how close it was to having heard all of it by yourself. (100-101)*

Kathy only includes this ritual in her narrative to set the scene for an unconnected incident, but its strangeness lingers; it's not how *we* listen to music.

* There's also the fact that in this version of Britain children are generated in labs, reared as cattle and routinely butchered for their vital organs.

Often the discord can be heard, faintly, in Kathy's language. Here she is, for example, describing how boys would proposition her at the Cottages: "Sometimes it was because he was interested in becoming a couple with you; other times it was just for a one-nighter" (125). Her language here is *slightly* off: where she says "was interested in becoming a couple with you", we might say "wanted to go out with you"; where she says, "it was just for a one-nighter" we might say, "it was just a one-night stand". It's not how we talk.

These details are easy to miss, and not obviously significant in themselves – maybe this is just how Kathy speaks – but their cumulative effect can't be ignored. We feel that these characters don't quite see as we see, live as we live. The glitches add up to a world which may resemble ours closely, but which doesn't feel right.

The writer Louis Menand writes interestingly about this feeling. "Ishiguro does not write like a realist," he says,

> he writes like someone impersonating a realist... It's realism from an instruction manual: literal, thorough, determined to leave nothing out. But it has a vaguely irreal effect.

A vaguely irreal effect: what Menand is describing is something which psychoanalysts and cultural theorists have spent much of the last century or so puzzling over: "the uncanny" (a rough translation of the German word *unheimliche*, which literally means "unhomely").

In an influential essay, "The Uncanny", Sigmund Freud describes the uncanny as "that species of the frightening that goes back to what was once well known and had long been familiar". More recently, in his book *The Uncanny* (2003), the cultural critic Nicholas Royle identifies the sources of the uncanny as, amongst other things,

> a peculiar commingling of the familiar and the unfamiliar... It can take the form of something familiar unexpectedly arising in a strange and unfamiliar context, or of something strange and unfamiliar unexpectedly arising in a familiar context. It can consist in a sense of homeliness uprooted, the revelation of something unhomely at the heart of hearth and home.... The uncanny can be felt in... manifestations of insanity or other forms of what might appear merely mechanical or automatic life... And conversely or likewise, it can be felt in response to dolls and other lifelike or mechanical objects... [It may] be construed as a foreign body within oneself, even the experience of oneself as a foreign body...

Unknowingly, Kathy offers her own vivid description of the uncanny when she remembers arriving at the Cottages after leaving Hailsham:

> *We could see hills in the distance that reminded us of the ones in the distance at Hailsham, but they seemed to us oddly crooked, like when you draw a picture of a friend and it's almost right but not quite, and the face on the sheet gives you the creeps. (116)*

This is a good description of the world depicted in *Never Let Me Go*: nearly an exact likeness of ours, but *not quite right*: vaguely irreal. It gives you the creeps.

"In telling a story," wrote the 19th century German psychiatrist Ernst Jentsch, in a comment Freud quotes and which seems particularly pertinent to Ishiguro's novel,

> one of the most successful devices for easily creating uncanny effects is to leave the reader in uncertainty as to whether a particular figure in the story is a human being or an automaton* and to do it in such a way that his attention is not focused directly upon his uncertainty, so that he may not be led to go into the matter and clear it up immediately.

In the 1970s, a Japanese robotics professor called Masahiro Mori put forward an idea that echoes Jentsch's comment and haunts *Never Let Me Go*. Mori observed that the more lifelike and human a robot becomes, the more unfamiliar it feels. A

* An early robot.

robot that is perfectly lifelike in every respect except that it doesn't blink, for example, *feels* more unsettlingly unfamiliar than a robot that looks nothing like a human being. Mori labelled the point at which the robot is so lifelike that it becomes frighteningly unfamiliar the "uncanny valley".*

Though they are not robots, the students of Hailsham seem to fall within the uncanny valley**: there's a strange feeling throughout the novel that they aren't quite human. An encounter they have with Madame illustrates this. Ruth suggests that Madame never acknowledges them because she's afraid of them. To test her theory, the children decide that, next time they see her, they will "swarm" around her and watch how she reacts. When they do so, Madame stops in her tracks. This is how Kathy describes the moment:

> *As she came to a halt, I glanced quickly at her face – as did the others, I'm sure. And I can still see it now, the shudder she seemed to be suppressing, the real dread... (35)*

The repressed shudder: this is a good description of the shiver-down-the-spine feeling you get when you experience something uncanny. As Madame's

* So called because of a dip in the graph measuring human likeness against familiarity.
** Hailsham itself lies literally in a valley.

response shows, there's something about these characters, stuck in the chilly shade of the uncanny valley, that stops people regarding them as quite human and which makes them seem very strange indeed.

Is there some sense in which they *are* robots, artificial intelligence? After all, they have been invented, constructed, engineered, tinkered with, *built*. And they have a mechanical function: not to live but to allow others to live. Aren't they just sophisticated life support machines? There's some evidence that they see themselves this way, at least. When, at the Cottages, they hear about the possibility of a deferral, Tommy believes he needs to produce soul-revealing art in order to be granted one. Having never been good at art at school, he starts drawing a series of bizarre animal pictures. This is how Kathy remembers them:

> *The first impression was like one you'd get if you took the back off a radio set: tiny canals, weaving tendons, miniature screws and wheels were all drawn with obsessive precision, and only when you held the page away could you see it was some kind of armadillo. (184-5)*

Is this what Tommy sees when he looks into his soul: a strange mechanical animal, an uncanny automaton, a machine?

Louis Menand has an interesting take on this

passage. He writes that it "almost certainly derives from Henri Bergson's famous definition of comedy: the mechanical encrusted on the living. The creatures Tommy draws are imagined versions of himself." Menand is right to link the uncanny to the comic: Berson's description is very similar to Jentsch's definition of the uncanny as a confusion between human and automaton. The writer Wyndham Lewis puts it slightly differently: "The root of the Comic is to be sought in the observations of a *thing* behaving like a person," he writes in *The Wild Body*. A cabbage reading Flaubert or a pair of waltzing trees are two of his examples. Lewis makes the link between the comic and the uncanny, too, when, quoting the philosopher William James, he says that the comic defamiliarises the human body to the extent that one comes to think of it as a "queer bodily shape in the darkness (a thing to make children scream at, as Stevenson says)". There's humour in the clones' strangeness.

They have a comic precursor in Ishiguro's oeuvre: the butler Stevens in *The Remains of the Day*. Stevens tries to behave at all times in the *correct* way as a butler: unobtrusively. But when, late in life, he gets a new boss, Mr Farrady, and Farraday starts conversing with him in a more light-hearted, "bantering" way than he's used to, Stevens doesn't know how to respond. Realising that simply smiling "in the correct manner" is inadequate, Stevens plucks up the courage to try to engage in the "banter". One morning, having been woken up by "a pair of gypsies gathering unwanted iron" and making a lot of noise, Farraday asks: "I suppose it wasn't you making that crowing noise this morning, Stevens?" Having a crack at a joke, Stevens responds: "More like swallows than crows, I would have said, sir. From the migratory aspect" (17). Mr Farraday is bemused. Stevens's response is not funny; his failure to interact naturally with another human is.

The impression is not unlike that of a robot trying to make a joke: a thing behaving like a person. Stevens's response may have all the *correct* elements of humour – it might be *the required sort of reply* – but there's something missing. The implication is that there's something ineffable and instinctive about humour: it can't be machine-produced, logically assembled. Stevens's response is robotic and he doesn't get it quite right: he's not a convincing version of the thing he's imitating. Often in the novel, people in the outside world struggle to place him socially: "Couldn't make you out for a while, see," says one man he comes across, "'cause you talk *almost like* a gentleman." Stevens is *almost like* a gentleman; his joke is *almost like* a joke; the clones at Hailsham are almost like people. The humour arises from their mechanical attempts to be exactly like: from their failed imitation.

Their failure is particularly pronounced because

15

they have limited material to imitate. They are totally isolated: "any place beyond Hailsham," Kathy tells us, "was like a fantasy land; we had only the haziest notions of the world outside" (66). Everything they know of the outside comes from the television – thus, Kathy notices of her friends, "so many of their mannerisms were copied from the television" (118). She notices, for example, how one of her friends has started rolling her eyes and saying "Gawd help us" like a character in their favourite sitcom. And even when she can't locate exactly the source of the mannerisms, she can guess. When Ruth starts to slap Tommy's arm with the back of her knuckles whenever she says goodbye, Kathy observes: "I'd not actually seen the slap on the elbow on the television, but I was pretty sure that's where the idea had come from" (119).

"Ishiguro's characters," Menand writes, are

> mad, compulsive, quasi-mechanical... There is something animatronic about them. They are simulators of humanness, figures engineered to pass as "real". What it means to be really a human is always a problem for them. Can you just copy other people? Would that take care of it?

This is a big question. That the clones are *not quite right*, that they are both uncanny and funny, that they are off-to-the-side and vaguely irreal, allows the novel to speculate, as we"ll see, on big existential questions. As Ishiguro has said, in an interview promoting the film of the book:

> One of the real advantages of using clones or robots or super computers... in fiction is that it immediately raises the question: what does it mean to be human? If these things are so close to being human, are they human? And you get back to some of these old, old questions that you find in the history of literature: what is a soul? What does it mean to have a soul?

Whether they can be considered human or not, one thing's certain: Ishiguro's characters are not functioning members of society. They aren't like us, they don't fit in. They're displaced, homeless, subjugated, orphaned, all of the above. In his book *Kazuo Ishiguro,* the critic Barry Lewis argues that Ishiguro's main subject is in fact homelessness. Ishiguro's characters, Lewis says, are constantly striving for "dignity"* and "to be dignified is to be "at home" with oneself and one's circumstances... Underlying all [Ishiguro's] books is a tug-of-war between a sense of homelessness and being 'at home'." Ishiguro's characters are "no longer at home with themselves"; they "live in houses that are not quite homes". They are homeless –

* This is the word Stevens uses in *The Remains of the Day:* perfect professionalism, for Stevens, means "dignity in keeping with [one's] position".

unhomed – *unheimliche* – uncanny.

The critic Cynthia F. Wong agrees. Quoting the great cultural theorist György Lukács, she writes,

> all fictional utterances represent "homesickness [or the expression of] the urge to be at home everywhere". As a kind of writer of exile, Ishiguro keenly and sympathetically portrays people searching for their souls and a way to feel at home despite their pain.

Wong goes further than Lewis: not only are Ishiguro's characters in some sense homeless, she argues, but they are, in some sense, orphans – they suffer from "failures of guardianship".

Condemned to live in institutions all their lives with no parents, the clones in *Never Let Me Go* are Ishiguro's most fully realised homeless orphans. They are not even at home in their own bodies: they belong to the state. Their organs will end up housed elsewhere. Their homelessness is total. And so is their orphanhood: they haven't *lost* their parents, they never had them to begin with. No one gave birth to them; they are not born. As John Mullan says, "Milton's Satan fantasised about being self-begot, and this is what Kathy H. and her fellow "students" are cursed to be". They have no ancestry and, Kathy implies, they have been genetically altered so that they can have no descendants. They are fleeting and unembedded:

Carey Mulligan (Kathy), Keira Knightley (Ruth) and Andrew Garfield (Tommy) in Mark Romanek's 2010 film adaptation of Never Let Me Go

they are, as Madame tells them at the end of the novel, by themselves (self-begot).

This is, perhaps, why they're not people like us. Human beings are social animals: our sense of ourselves comes from our interactions with others, from the people we look up to, from the people we don't, from how we think about our place in the world, from the vast matrix of social relations that constitutes our culture, our society, our environment. If we have no one to look up to, no parents, no ancestors, no origins, history, culture – if we are totally isolated from the outside world, then we can't place ourselves in the world, in society; we're on our own. This is what's happened to Ishiguro's clones.

But just because so many of the tools with which people fashion their identities have been denied them, it doesn't mean they're not human.* I want to go back to what Wyndham Lewis said about comedy: "The root of the Comic is to be sought in the observations of a *thing* behaving like a person." His definition doesn't actually end there. He goes on: "But from that point of view, all men are necessarily comic: for they are all things or physical bodies, behaving as *persons*." If the clones aren't human, if they're just things pretending to be humans, then so are we. Humanness, the novel suggests, is not constituted by "fitting in", by being like everyone else: humanness is something irreducible that comes before individual identity. As the critic Sarak Kerr writes,

> The dare Ishiguro has taken on might be this: to capture what is unmistakably human, what survives and insists on subtly expressing itself after you subtract the big stuff – the specific baggage, the parents, orientation towards a culture, a past and possible futures, that shapes people into individuals.

If Ishiguro's characters are only *almost* like us, it's not because they're in some way genetically or biologically deficient. It's nurture, not nature. And

* Of course, they're not human really – they're words on a page, fictional utterances – but that's another debate.

indeed, it's wrong to see them as *almost like*. Through reading the novel, we come to accept them as different rather than deficient: the same, but different. We're as *almost like* them as they are *almost like* us. They are products of their own environment: thus they have their own customs, habits, rituals, mythologies and beliefs that don't extend beyond the walls of Hailsham. Once we come to terms with that, we begin to see how like us they actually are (but more of that later). This makes *Never Let Me Go* a great lesson in overcoming racial prejudices.

The Familiar

Kathy's writing style is drably familiar, cultivated from the tissue of cliché. On the first page alone she uses the phrases "waste of space"; "I'm not trying to boast; "I do know for a fact"; "by and large"; "it means a lot to me"; "snap out of it"; "don't get half the credit"; "pick and choose"; "get peoples' backs up" (3). Elsewhere, she is "with" her donors "every step of the way" (4); she is "in hot water with" Miss Emily (44); amorous couples are "going at it left, right and centre" (95).

Kathy H. is no literary stylist. Her writing has all the naivety and lack of sophistication of a bad school essay, totally without subtlety and nuance.

She is constantly explaining – "I should explain why I got so bothered by Ruth saying what she did..." (124), joining sections together inexpertly – "But to explain what we were talking about that evening, I'll have to go back a little bit" (188), underlining her intentions – "What happened after that row over the chess illustrates pretty well the point I'm making" (52), and drearily laying bare her narrative logic –"So that was the background... and you can maybe see now why..." (143). If this were a piece of homework it would inevitably be returned with the words "Show, don't tell!" scrawled at the top of the page.

Some critics baulk at the ordinariness of Kathy's voice: the late, great Frank Kermode thought the novel's "dear-diary prose surely reduces one's interest" and makes the book "a failure". Others regard it as key to the novel's success – Margaret Attwood, for one:

> Ishiguro's tone is perfect: Kathy... prattles on in the obsessive manner touchy girls have, going back over past conversations and registering every comment and twitch and crush and put-down and cold shoulder and gang-up and spat.

I think Attwood is right: the book needs a banal narrator. Because, despite the extremity of their situation, *Never Let Me Go* is in many ways a novel *about* banality. It is in the realm of the banal that it finds its narrative energy.

Ruth's pencil case is a case in point. It appears out of nowhere one day, and Ruth wants (or so Kathy thinks) everyone to believe it was a present to her from Miss Geraldine, their favourite guardian, though she probably bought it at a Sale. It's a completely ordinary object yet it takes up five pages (the fervour it elicits, the jealousy it provokes, the tensions it causes) – about five more than are given to explaining the outlandish specifics of their situation.

Partly, this is because Ishiguro wants to show us the reality of his characters' everyday lives. But it goes deeper than that. His characters are unusually *drawn* to the banal. Here is Kathy describing something she notices on the wall in a Norfolk greasy spoon:

> *There was one cardboard notice pinned over the counter that had been done in coloured felt-tips, and at the top of it was the word "look" with a staring eye drawn inside each "o". I see the same thing so often these days I don't even register it, but back then I hadn't seen it before. So I was looking at it admiringly... (147)*

Doesn't that "so" say so much? As if this naff poster is an obvious source of wonder. Kathy's esteem in the banal continues to the end of her life, when she develops an obsession with desk lamps. "Here in my bedsit," she boasts.

> *I've got these four desk-lamps, each a different colour, but all the same design – they have these ribbed necks you can bend whichever way you want. So I might go looking for a shop with another lamp like that in its window – not to buy, but just to compare with my ones at home. (204)*

Again, "so" says it all.

For the clones, there is something soothing about the trite, the ordinary. Kathy describes how she likes to visit regional branches of Woolworths:

> *I like places like that: a large store with lots of aisles displaying bright plastic toys, greeting cards, loads of cosmetics, maybe even a photo booth. Today, if I'm in a town and find myself with some time to kill, I'll stroll into somewhere just like that, where you can hang around and enjoy yourself, not buying a thing, and the assistants don't mind at all. (155)*

In all these examples, though commerce is the emphasis, Kathy isn't interested in making a purchase: she just wants to soak up the atmosphere. Here, it's as if the shop is a temple to the ordinary, a place in which she can take time out of her hectic schedule driving round the country, mopping up blood, to worship the banal.

Banality is what they dream of, too. One of their

favourite games at the Cottages is to pretend that they will lead long and fulfilling lives and describe their fantasy lives to each other. "I don't remember anyone saying they were going to be a movie star or anything like that," Kathy says. "The talk was more likely to be about becoming a postman or working on a farm. Quite a few students wanted to be drivers of one sort or other..." (140). Ruth has a particularly fervent fantasy about working in a drab office with lots of pot plants. This is the best they can imagine for themselves. It sounds thrilling.

For the clones, banality has the status of novelty. Stuck in their absurd situation, it represents something they'll never be: normal. Where we might read fantasy or science fiction novels as a kind of escapism, these characters – who are *in* a science fiction novel – find their escape in dreams of a banal life. Their dreams allow them to forget who they are.

Similarly, the banal objects they covet give them a surface on to which they can unload fears and desires that would otherwise be so strong they'd drive them mad. Barry Lewis writes about how significant Freud's idea of *displacement* is to Ishiguro. "Freud chose this term," he writes,

> to designate the... process that diverts the attention of the psyche away from potentially damaging material. Fears and forbidden desires

are masked by their association with relatively trifling symbols, objects or situations.

Ruth's pencil case is significant because, as we've seen, she wants the other children to think she has been given it by their favourite guardian, as if it's a physical demonstration of the parental love they will never receive: her deep desire to be cherished and loved and cared for are scrunched up and zipped tight inside it. Kathy's tape – the one with the song "Never Let Me Go" on it – has a similar role. If she can load her fear of death and abandonment onto a phrase sung by an old singer on a dusty old cassette, then she can keep it shut away.

Kathy's language enacts a similar kind of displacement, making manageable the unmanageable. In Wai-chew Sim's words, it "consistently tones down, dampens, or makes banal its potentially lurid material". Think of all the euphemisms the characters use. As the critic Mark Currie writes, their vocabulary

> names as "guardians", "training", "students", "carers", "donations", "deferrals", and "completion" a brutal reality more properly named as captors, socialization, clones, prefects, enforced organ donations, false hope and death.

The sanitised language hides the true horror of their situation. At the beginning of the novel,

Kathy, describing coming to the end of her stint as a carer, says: "it feels just about right to be finishing at last come the end of the year" (4). A first time reader would never suspect she was describing her own impending death; with her flattened language – which is "untormented", says John Mullan, "by the knowledge of what will happen to her" – she can pretend to herself that she isn't.

By worshipping the trite and dreaming of the ordinary, the clones are able to pretend that there's nothing unusual about them, that everything's fine, they aren't being mistreated, death isn't coming. The banality makes acceptable and bearable the atrocious.

But Kathy's writing is not just bland: it's bad. John Mullan describes her voice as "deprived", "ineloquent" and laments her "struggles with narration". The academic Sebastian Groes complains about her "exhausted vocabulary, uncomplicated sentences and inability to express complicated emotions". For the novelist David Lodge, her prose lacks "wit, sensuousness and originality".

She can be annoyingly wordy: when Tommy is about to die, for example, she writes: "*What I'm saying is that all in all I was under the impression* we were dealing with the fourth donation pretty well together..." (274): the italicised words (my emphasis) just don't need to be there. Occasionally she tries her hand at poetic scene-setting but can't pull it off: "Anyway, once you came out to the pond, you'd find a tranquil atmosphere waiting, with ducks and bulrushes and pond-weed." (25) She misuses language: "Maybe I'm exaggerating it, but my memory is that for a whole class to fit into that room, students literally had to pile on top of each other" (56). If students *literally* piled on top of each other, though, it would be an odd scene indeed. She repeats herself clumsily: "we couldn't decide whether *or not* the guardians wanted us to have sex *or not*" (94).

And it's not just the writing that fails: her memory repeatedly lets her down. Her narrative abounds with qualifiers like "from what I remember" (15) or "My guess is" (46). "This was all a long time ago," she says towards the start, "so I might have some of it wrong; but my memory is that..." (13) How can we trust her memories? How can we be sure she isn't making it up? At one point, she as good as admits that she is: "Tommy didn't quite put it this way but I'm sure that's how it happened" (19). She even doubts her own powers of recall: "Years later, I gently hinted this to Ruth, and she didn't seem to know what I was talking about, so maybe I was wrong" (188).

As Mark Currie has seen, Kathy's memories aren't even totally her own:

> Her characteristic phrases such as, "That was when..." and "There was the time when..." suggest

> a kind of foreknowledge of the events to be narrated, or a community of addressees for whom these events, or the stories of them, are already known. Everything has been told before, and there has often been a collective agreement on a particular version of events.

Kathy, Tommy and Ruth, in other words, have gone over their memories again and again, and, finding that they remember things differently, have collectively rewritten their past. But a consensus hasn't always been reached:

> *I'm not sure when the big temper tantrums started. My own memory of it is that Tommy was always known for his temper, even in the Infants, but he claimed to me they only began after the teasing got bad. (20-1)*

Or, later: "When I mentioned how I'd sometimes seen the head wandering around Hailsham in a dream, talking to herself, Ruth took offence, saying: "She was never like that!" (43). "Okay," Kathy says after bitching about her friends Chrissie and Rodney, "I'm maybe being a bit hard on these two. When I was remembering them with Tommy not so long ago, he thought they were pretty decent people" (140).

"Memory," says the narrator of Ishiguro's first novel, *A Pale View of Hills*, Etsuko,

> can be an unreliable thing; often it is heavily coloured by the circumstances in which one remembers, and no doubt this applies to certain of the recollections I have gathered here.

It applies to the recollections Kathy has gathered, too: "if these incidents now seem full of significance," she says, "it's probably because I'm looking at them in the light of what came later" (77). Whatever the accuracy of her memories, Kathy redraws their significance to meet her present needs: as we'll see in the next chapter, the circumstances in which she remembers colour her memories almost literally.

We should be alert to Etusko's use of the word "unreliable". Ishiguro has made a career out of writing variations on the "unreliable narrator" – a term coined by the American literary critic Wayne C. Booth to refer to those narrators who deliberately lie to, or withhold crucial information from, their addressees. But Kathy isn't quite like that. If she wants to keep things unsaid, it's because they're too painful to bring to the surface. She's lying to herself, not to us. "She is not," John Mullan says, "so much an unreliable narrator, as an inadequate narrator."

Unreliable narrators are fun to read – often villainous, they keep the reader guessing and the reading process becomes a game of cat and mouse: the reader becomes detective. But an inadequate

FIVE FACTS ABOUT
Kazuo Ishiguro & *Never Let Me Go*

1.

In 2015, The University of Texas paid over $1m (£635,000) for Ishiguro's extensive archive of notes and unpublished work, including multiple drafts of *Never Let Me Go*.

2.

Alex Garland, who wrote the screenplay for the film adaptation of *Never Let Me Go*, drafted the script and approached producers before the book was even published.

3.

Six out of seven of Ishiguro's novels have been shortlisted for major literary awards, including the Man Booker Prize (three times).

4.

In his teens, Ishiguro planned to be a singer-songwriter. "I used to see myself as some sort of musician type but there came a point when I thought: actually, this isn't me at all. I'm much less glamorous. I'm one of these people with corduroy jackets with elbow patches. It was a real comedown."

5.

Never Let Me Go ranked number 18 on *Time Magazine*'s '100 Best English-language Novels from 1923 to 2005'.

narrator is something different. An inadequate narrator is simply inadequate. Kathy's memories are inaccurate and she can't express them anyway.

So what's in it for us? Why does Ishiguro want us to spend so much time with a bad and boring writer? It's because he wants us to look beneath the surface of the writing. The failure of Kathy's writing project signals to the reader that she isn't in control of her own story, and that the real story exists elsewhere. Ishiguro is telling us to read between the lines, to be alert to the unsaid and buried – to appreciate that, as the novelist Salmon Rushdie puts it, "just below the understatement of [the] surface is a turbulence as immense as it is slow".

"I'm interested in the way words hide meaning," Ishiguro has said, and it's a remarkable aspect of his books that he can convey his meaning by deliberately not conveying it, that he can make a whole other text visible behind the real one – "unexpressed," as M. John Harrison puts it, "but perfectly articulated". In an Ishiguro novel, in the words of his teacher, the novelist Malcolm Bradbury, the narrative "hides behind itself, forcing the reader persistently to unlock it". "Few writers," Mark Karmine has written, "dare to say so little of what they mean as Ishiguro." The true meaning and emotional heft of Kathy's narration is not what she says, badly – it's what Ishiguro doesn't say, well.

Bored by her prose, alert to the inconsistencies

of her narration and her inadequacy as a narrator, the reader's focus shifts from *what* Kathy's narrating to *why* she's narrating. What's she really trying to achieve, the reader starts to ask, by going through her life story? Why tell it at all?

Making the Strange Familiar

Ishiguro's narrators are united in their apparent desire to understand themselves, which they claim motivates their narration. They tell their stories not so much to us as to themselves in an attempt to gain a clearer picture of who they are, where they are and how they got there. "I've been getting the urge to order all these old memories," Kathy says, because "I realise now just how much of what occurred later came out of our time at Hailsham" (37).

But that doesn't feel quite right, does it? It might be the case, as Cynthia F. Wong puts it, that "Kathy return[s] to [her] memories of childhood in order to understand the basis of her present isolation." But, as we've seen, Kathy's attempts at self-narration are seriously lacking. As Wong also understands, although Kathy seeks truth, she "find[s] multiple ways of dismantling access to it, because of the painfulness of truth itself".

She seems too quick to interpret her own

narration; she over-explains, over-interprets, over-clarifies – all of which suggests self-deception rather than self-knowledge. One of the most apparent symptoms of her self-deception is that she repeatedly gets distracted, digresses at length, and expresses surprise about where she ends up. After a strange encounter with Miss Emily, for example, she says: "But that's not really what I want to talk about just now. What I want to do now is get a few things down about Ruth" (45). But is that really what she wants to do now? The reader suspects not. Over and again, Ishiguro shows us how lacking Kathy's interpretations of her own narrative intentions are, while showing us that truthful interpretations don't really matter to her. She imagines, for example, that the song "Never Let Me Go" is about

> *a woman who'd been told she couldn't have babies, who'd really, really wanted them all her life. Then there's a sort of miracle and she has a baby and she holds this baby very close to her and walks around singing: "Baby, never let me go... [But e]ven at the time, I realised this couldn't be right, that this interpretation didn't fit with the rest of the lyrics. But that wasn't an issue with me. (70)*

The effect of the interpretation is what matters, not its truth.

Just as she embraces her own erroneous

interpretations of events, Kathy misses – or deliberately ignores – details that seem vital to any possibility of a full understanding of herself. For example, while describing a confrontation with Tommy after one of his temper tantrums, she lets something slip:

> *my approaching Tommy that afternoon was part of a phase I was going through around that time – something to do with compulsively setting myself challenges – and I'd more or less forgotten all about it when Tommy stopped me a few days later.* (13)

Her compulsive setting of challenges for herself – buried in a parenthesis and dismissed with the phrase, "something to do with..." – is never mentioned again, never interrogated. If Kathy really wanted to examine her past unflinchingly, she would need to scrutinise such details. As it is, she seems to want to – but can't quite – bury her past. Kathy is part of a long line of narrators in Ishiguro's novels, then, who, though they claim to be motivated by a desire for self-knowledge, don't really know themselves and, one suspects, don't really want to. "How deeply their self-estrangement runs," says Cynthia F. Wong.

In which case, the question remains: why is Kathy telling her story?

For Ishiguro, the past is not a "foreign country", as L.P. Hartley famously proclaimed. As

Christopher Banks, the narrator of *When We Were Orphans*, says of his childhood: "it's hardly a foreign land to me. In many ways, it's where I've continued to live all my life". Banks, an orphan whose parents mysteriously disappeared, spends much of his childhood pretending to be a detective looking for them. In later life, he becomes the most celebrated detective in the world, and it becomes clear that his solving of crimes is a displaced attempt to find his parents. Ishiguro's point is that adult identity is built on childhood belief.

He makes the same point in *Never Let Me Go*. The clones learn about the counties of England through old photos that Miss Emily shows them in "Geography" lessons. When Kathy visits those counties for the first time in her twenties, she still sees them through Miss Emily's lens: "it's amazing," she says, "the extent to which my idea of the various counties is still set by these pictures miss Emily put up on her easel" (65). What Kathy is taught at school literally structures the way she sees the world as an adult.

We've seen how the clones' isolation has led to them creating their own mythology. One significant aspect of this mythology – the idea of Norfolk as a kind of spiritual lost property zone – stems from this same geography lesson. Because Norfolk is "stuck out here on the east", Miss Emily tells them,

It's not on the way to anywhere. People... bypass it altogether. For that reason, it's a peaceful corner of England, rather nice. But it's also something of a lost corner. (65)

And because they have their own "Lost Corner" on the third floor, a lost property cupboard, this idea resonates with them. After the lesson, someone claims that "what Miss Emily had said was that Norfolk was England's "lost corner", where all the lost property found in the country ended up" (65). Kathy knows this is a ridiculous proposition, yet belief in it endures and grows. Later in life, when she and Tommy find another copy of the tape she lost as a child in Norfolk, she says, "we both felt deep down some tug, some old will to believe again in something that was once close to our hearts" (66). At the end of the novel, after Tommy's death, Kathy describes getting out of her car in the Norfolk countryside and watching some old rubbish caught in a barbed wire fence rustling in the wind. "I started to imagine just a little fantasy thing," she tells us.

I half-closed me eyes and imagined this was the spot where everything I'd ever lost since my childhood had washed up, and I was now standing here in front of it, and if I waited long enough, a tiny figure would appear on the horizon across the field, and gradually get larger until I'd see it was Tommy, and he'd wave, maybe even call. (282)

Even at the end, her inner life is structured by Miss Emily's lesson about the English counties.

Kathy's "will to believe" is crucial. It conquers her scepticism. As with their enduring belief in deferrals, the myth about Norfolk allows them to hold on to the idea of something beyond death, a kind of afterlife. And that the Norfolk myth keeps returning, despite the knowledge that it's make-believe, shows the extent to which Kathy's adult identity is continuous with her childhood fantasy. Like her interpretation of her favourite song, Kathy knows it isn't true, but a kind of emotional belief in it keeps her going. The novel speaks of the human need to create illusions knowingly and then do all we can not to dispel them.

For Ishiguro, we are what we remember. But what we remember isn't necessarily what happened: how we remember is to some extended based on who we are. Identity comes from memory, but memory comes from identity. On this confusing, dizzying subject, Wai-chew Sim quotes the academic Christoph Henke. "Henke argues," Sim writes,

> that [memory and identity] are co-implicated or co-extensive with each other... he states tellingly that, "The core meaning of any individual or group identity, namely, a sense of sameness over

time and space, is sustained by remembering; and what is remembered is defined by assumed identity." According to Henke... "remembering is a complex process which bears no direct relation to the events experienced in the past." The individual's "inner story" is structured in response to present needs and "undergoes continual rewriting and editing". It entails "a continual self-creation" of the ego.

This is an important thought. What Sim is implying is that, by ordering her memories, by telling her story, Kathy is not trying to understand herself, but *to create herself.*

So what kind of self is Kathy trying to create and why? The sun casts some light on the answer. At Hailsham, the sun is always shining. Anecdotes begin with phrases like, "We were in Room 7 on a sunny winter's morning" (32) or "I was doing this little walk one sunny evening" (44) or "It was a morning of brilliant sunshine" (88). Once they leave Hailsham, the weather gets worse: anecdotes now begin with phrases like "We'd just had one of those summer days of rain and thunderstorms" (195), or "The particular morning I'm talking about, it was really foggy..." (275).

It seems unlikely that the sun was *always* shining at Hailsham, and *never* afterwards, so we begin to suspect that the sunshine is an invention of Kathy's memory, a product of nostalgia. It's as if, wanting to remember Hailsham as a golden time, she literally colours it golden: "The early years... they tend to blur into each other as a kind of golden time, and when I think about them at all, even the not-so-great things, I can't help feeling a sort of glow" (76). There are plenty of "not-so-great things" at Hailsham, but most of them – their isolation, their yearning for parental love, their confusion about who they are, their fear, their anxieties – we are left to intuit, to perceive behind the cracks in the narrative.

Kathy doesn't want to break the spell of childhood. Promoting the novel, Ishiguro spoke regularly of the necessary deception involved in bringing up children: "Certainly, when my daughter was younger," he said in an interview for *NPR Radio*,

> I tried to keep her in a bubble sealed off from the realities of the world that actually awaited her... It struck me how quickly even total strangers would enter into the conspiracy with myself and my wife... Everybody wanted to censor out the sadness of the world. They desperately wanted this little child to be deceived about how nice a place the world was.

He was struck by the "idea that in order to have a proper childhood, an element of deception must be used" and that, "to make [a] childhood work, you

Kazuo Ishiguro (above) was born in Nagasaki, Japan, in 1954 but has lived in Britain since 1960

have to deceive [children] into believing it's all worthwhile." This is precisely what the teachers of Hailsham are trying to do: to deceive the clones into believing it's all worthwhile.

The creation of a falsely idyllic childhood does not constitute, for Ishiguro, a meaningless lie – it is an act of moral and political positivity. Carrying a false picture, a fiction, of a good world from childhood through adulthood – from childhood deception through to adult nostalgia – is, he says, "a way of holding in your memory a picture of a better world than the one we find ourselves in". At one point in *When We Were Orphans*, Christopher Banks says: "We mustn't get too nostalgic for childhood." He is cradling a dying soldier whom he believes to be a childhood friend; this character shakes his head and says,

> Important. Very important. Nostalgic. When we nostalgic we remember. A world better than this world we discover when we grow. We remember and wish good world come back again. So very important.

If we can *remember* a better world, in other words, we can hope for a better world.

For Kathy, the need to believe in a better world has a particular urgency. She has no parents, she has no history, she will have no children. John Mullan says: "When nothing of a person extends back before them, memory is all they have... Their past is entirely their own, to be reclaimed or to disappear, or perhaps to be created." If Kathy can hold on to the memory of a happy childhood, whether real or not, she is able to imagine a better world – a world in which people aren't built in labs, torn open and redistributed: a world in which she is cared for and her life has had some meaning, in which she is considered fully human. Hailsham, as Wai-chew Sim puts it, "functions as a symbol of hope, of the human need for sustaining stories and dreams".

The combination of the falsely idyllic childhood that Miss Emily creates for her and the sustaining of that fiction through a nostalgic retelling of her past, allows Kathy to (attempt to) normalise the strange horror she is to live through. It allows her to think of herself as more of a normal citizen, leading to a life which is perhaps deluded but which is nevertheless happier and more hopeful than the life she otherwise would have led. It allows her to foster a belief, though she knows it's a fantasy, in something beyond her impending death. It allows her to be a happier person – to be a person full stop. It gives her the will to believe in herself.

Kathy has a lot to be thankful for: Hailsham is a gift. When she and Tommy confront Miss Emily and discover that they can't "defer", they accuse her of misleading the students, hiding the true nature of their lives from them. "Yes, in many ways we *fooled* you," Miss Emily says.

> *I suppose you could even call it that. But we sheltered you during those years, and we gave you your childhood... You built your lives on what we gave you. You wouldn't be who you are today if we'd not protected you. You wouldn't have become absorbed in your lessons, you wouldn't have lost yourselves in your art and your writing. Why should you have done, knowing what lay in store for each of you? You would have told us it was all pointless, and how could we have argued with you? (263)*

Sunshine is important: it's what were built on.

Making the Familiar Strange

Just a few weeks after *Never Let Me Go* was published, cinemas started playing a trailer for a new film called *The Island*. The film, directed by Michael Bay (of *Transformers* fame) follows Lincoln Six Echo (Ewan McGregor) and Jordan Two Delta (Scarlet Johansson), who live in a strange, clinical institution which keeps them healthy at all costs. They have a routine, isolated existence. Their world looks like ours, but it has odd customs, rituals, mythologies. Lincoln and Jordan clearly fancy each other but are held apart by the institution's rules and restrictions. They know nothing of the outside world, but as they grow older they start to question what they've been told about who they are. They discover that they are clones who have been created for the sole purpose of growing spare organs. They, and everyone they know, will die young.

As a set up, it couldn't be more similar to *Never Let Me Go*; as a story, however, it couldn't be more different. Bay's film is full of chase sequences, explosions, suspense and sex. Lincoln and Jordan escape, go on the run, and return to liberate their fellow clones. It ends with the mastermind of the operation being killed, the institution blown up, the clones storming into the real world, and

McGregor and Johansson sailing off into the sunset. In *Never Let Me Go* things carry on as normal, nothing is disturbed, nothing changes, no one runs away, no one rises up in rebellion; the characters passively accept their gruesome fate. *The Island* is an extremely loud film but the absence of all that noise in *Never Let Me Go* is deafening.

There are several reasons for the lack of rebellion and resistance that we would expect in a dystopian tale. Partly, it's because Ishiguro wants to remain within the realms of everyday experience. However outlandish his subject, he wants his novel to feel like real life, not like a Hollywood movie. His flattening out of the narrative landscape brings his fantastical characters closer to our world: it makes them more like us. But it does the opposite, too. The everydayness of Ishiguro's novel makes it easier for us to put ourselves in its characters' shoes: we don't know how we would feel if we were on the run in the desert with the FBI chasing us, but we can imagine what it would be like to be a child fussing over a pencil case, to have a favourite song, to take pride in an artwork we've produced, to be jealous of our best friend, to fall in love. For all the strangeness of its set-up, the weird customs and rituals it portrays, and the unfamiliar vocabulary it employs, *Never Let Me Go* works by drawing us into its world.

Ishiguro employs many strategies to achieve the

effect. By hiding the truth of his texts behind the veil of his narrators' words, for example, he clouds the reading so that we are, as Wai-chew Sim has it, "in the same condition as the narrator, struggling to find a 'truth' behind the filter of [her] memory". Similarly, what Mark Currie refers to as the "hermeneutic puzzle"* that results from the many competing interpretations of events the novel presents, is a "prism" into which the reader is "invited".

And there's the bizarre way Ishiguro's narrators talk to their imagined readers. They address them as if they're a part of what they're narrating, as if they exist in their world. "Of course, you may be new to this city..." says the narrator Ono on the first page of *An Artist in the Floating World*. "You will no doubt agree," the butler Stevens suggests in *The Remains of the Day*, "that the hardest of situations as regards dinner-waiting is when there are just two diners present." Repeatedly, Kathy begins sentences with the phrase "I don't know how it was where you were, but at Hailsham...", implying that her reader, too, was brought up in an organ-farming institution.

At first, we might feel alienated. This isn't for us. We aren't like them, we don't know what they're talking about; we're eavesdropping. But as we grow accustomed to the narration, as we're drawn further in, a strange thing starts to happen: we

* *Hermeneutic*: of, relating to, or concerning interpretation.

begin to suspect that we are like Kathy; that we *do* know what she's talking about. As John Mullan says, thinking of both *The Remains of the Day* and *Never Let Me Go*, it's "as if, at some deeper level, our recognition and sympathy as readers reveals that we are all butlers (and clones)".

"We begin the novel horrified by their difference from us," James Wood writes, "and end it thoughtful about their similarity to us." We begin to suspect that the novel's subject is not human cloning after all but, as Margaret Attwood has it, "ourselves, seen through a glass, darkly". *The Island* thinly makes a point about where our society is heading – it dramatises what might happen if we were to continue to develop science and chase profit without putting up ethical barriers. *Never Let Me Go* isn't totally unconcerned with those issues: as Wai-chew Sim argues, it

> relates the commodification of human beings to a culture where the demands of corporate profit-making penetrate all aspects of social life and trump all considerations... Only in such a society can a vast network of causes and forces culminate in human organs being put on a shelf like canned goods in a store.

But the main point Ishiguro wants to make is much closer to home, and his continual refusal of the dystopian science fiction genre (no breaking free, no happy-ever-after) makes this apparent to the reader.

The clones' lives, he has said, are "concertinaed" versions of our own. In a recent interview with the fantasy writer Neil Gaiman, he described how children are

> allowed a sanctioned world where fantasy and imagination is deemed to be fine, in fact, almost desirable... [But when they] get to a certain age, they have to start getting prepared to be units of the labour force. And so, society has to start getting the fantasy element out of children, so that they can become factory workers, soldiers, white-collar workers, whatever, because it's seen to be not useful to the overall economic enterprise to have children growing up maintaining that fantasy element. You don't want people who are too dreamy or who are imagining things: you want them to accept this is the nitty-gritty of real life, that they've just got to get on with it.

We can see how this might apply to the clones in *Never Let Me Go*. Like us, they are allowed to indulge in fantasy as children, seeing the world as a nicer place than it is (think, for example, of how we're encouraged to believe in Father Christmas*). They go to school, sit through lessons that have no

* "Why do I got to be the guy who tells the kids there's no Santa Claus?" asks Steve Buscemi's character in *The Island*, when revealing the truth to Lincoln and Jordan,

bearing on what they will end up doing; they go briefly out into the world as young adults, dreaming of lives they know they'll never live, before joining the labour force: becoming carers and ultimately giving up their bodies. Then they die.

Ishiguro's characters don't rebel, rise up, run away – don't even question the predicament they're in – because it doesn't occur to them to. It's what they know. In *The Island*, the institution is effectively a prison; in *Never Let Me Go*, there's no coercive force keeping the characters in line. Theirs is a prison without bars. "The chains that hold them in place are primarily ideological or mental," says Sim. They give up their organs because giving up organs is what they do. Think about the novel's title: *Never Let Me Go*. It's like "a request for everlasting captivity", in Mark Currie's words, and "provokes a question about why we might not only accept but actually beseech our own confinement". Like the clones, our paths are preordained: by and large we all of us go to school, grow up, work, die. We do so because it's what we do, because it's the system we're born into, because we can't cheat death.

What are we to make of the lack of resistance in the novel? We've seen how Ishiguro thinks a kind of knowing ignorance can be beneficial. But there's another side to that coin. Isn't it *better* to know? Shouldn't we heed the troublesome Miss Lucy, who wants to puncture the fantasy world of

Hailsham and tell the students the truth? "Your lives are set out for you," she says.

> *You were brought into this world for a purpose, and your futures, all of them, have been decided... If you're to have decent lives, you have to know who you are and what lies ahead of you, every one of you.* (79-80)

Shouldn't we condemn Hailsham, as M. John Harrison does, as an institution whose purpose is not to give the clones a basis for hope, but to "instil the powerful mechanisms of self-repression and denial that will keep them steady and dependable from one donation to the next"?

The clones seem to have internalised a negative image of themselves based on how they think society sees them: as disposable, trash. Pretty much everything they value – artworks, private collections, origins, dreams, each other – they refer to at one point or another as rubbish. Tommy describes his art as "rubbish"; (105) when she moves to the Cottages, Ruth describes her collection of Sales purchases as "rubbish" (129). In Norfolk, wondering where her genetic material might have come from, she screams: "We're modelled from *trash*... If you want to look for [possible origins], if you want to do it properly, then... You look in rubbish bins" (164). Later, shortly before Ruth is to "complete", she tells

Kathy about a dream she had of being back at Hailsham, which suggests that trash is what she feels comfortable amidst: "there I was," she says, "in Room 14, and I was looking out of the window and everything outside was flooded... And I could see rubbish floating by under my window, empty drink cartons, everything. It was nice and tranquil, just like it is here" (221). Trash is what she feels comfortable amidst. Finally, when Kathy imagines Tommy reappearing at the end of the novel, it is the sight of rubbish that inspires her sad fantasy, as if Tommy himself is resurfaced trash:

> *All along the fence... all sorts of rubbish had caught and tangled.... Up in the branches of the trees, too, I could see, flapping about, torn plastic sheeting and bits of old carrier bags... I was thinking about the rubbish, the flapping plastic in the branches, the shore-line of odd stuff caught along the fencing, and I half-closed my eyes and imagined... (282)*

Shouldn't we want the clones to fight against such a negative image of themselves rather than internalise it?

There are a number of critics who consider Kathy's passive chirpiness grossly unethical. For Victor Sage, the novel can be read "as an analogy of American slave culture", and Kathy's willingness as a carer, along with her positivity, show her to be complicit in the horrors of slavery. Sage goes further, arguing that "the novel also reworks the fascist logic that led to the advocacy of eugenics and, eventually, the obscenity of the concentration camps". In this light, Kathy's enthusiasm as a carer looks far more sinister. The critic Lydia R. Cooper goes as far as to compare her to the Nazi Adolf Eichmann, whose bureaucratic, administrative approach to the death camps moved the philosopher Hannah Arendt to coin the phrase "the banality of evil". Kathy's "acquiescence in the attitudes imposed on her by her society", Cooper writes, makes her, like Eichmann, "an enabler of the systematic murder of clones for their vital organs... Blindness and obedience... are dangerous values to uphold when such passive behaviour leads to atrocity". Tommy, with his rages and tantrums, is the more admirable character: his tantrums, for Cooper,

> are implicit rejections of the role to which he has been condemned and indicate an important level of autonomy... his fury suggests that, while the clones may not be able to control their physical destiny, they can control their emotional response.

I'm not wholly with Cooper – her argument seems a little excessive. But it's not without evidence. Ishiguro takes care to suggest the possibility of Kathy's complicity from the very first paragraph, in which she tells us that she has learnt "to shrug and tell [donors] to snap out of it" when they lament their lot (3). It's not a remark that would necessarily register on a first reading, but in light of what we learn later it casts a rather unpleasant shadow. A few pages later, she's complicit in bullying Tommy. A group of boys are teasing him – leading to one of his rages – and Kathy and her friends are watching from a window, laughing. She says: "whatever the boys chose to do was pretty remote from us; whether we approved or not didn't come into it" (7). Yet she's happy to sit back and watch.

The question of whether it is better to live in a dream world like Kathy, or to rage and kick and scream with conscious futility like Tommy, is one that Ishiguro deliberately leaves unanswered. He shows us the dangers of complicity, but he shows us, too, the importance of optimism. Whether the two positions can be reconciled or not, I think he wants to shift the debate. He wants to ask not how we should respond to the systems we are born into, to our unalterable fates, but how we should respond to each other within those systems: that, for Ishiguro, is what counts in our lives. And the resounding answer he gives to that question in all of his books is: we should be nice to each other.

Whether Hailsham encourages complicity or fosters a dynamic optimism, one thing it does for certain is teach the clones to be nice. It encourages happiness" (75). "I don't play it much," Kathy tells us, "because the music has nothing to do with anything." But, "now Ruth has gone, it's become one of my most precious possessions" (75). Once again, it is the kindness behind the act that makes the difference, not the act itself, which has "nothing to do with anything". The object is a kind of displaced metaphor (an "objective correlative", in T.S. Eliot's words) for Ruth's kindness. These acts of kindness – and there are many, many more – are beacons in their lives, which they carry forward and which make things look that little bit brighter. Lacking parents, they look after each other: they are each other's carers. And so, Ishiguro is saying, should we be.

That the deferral turns out to be a myth might suggest a pessimism on Ishiguro's part about the power of love. But what happens after Madame has dashed Kathy and Tommy's hopes suggests otherwise. On their drive home, Tommy asks Kathy to stop the car. Kathy does so and Tommy disappears into a nearby field. After a while, Kathy hears strange, animal-sounding cries coming from the field and realises that Tommy is raving and raging against the machine for the first time in years. She gets out of the car, finds him, puts her arms around him. "He tried to shake me off," she says,

but I kept holding on, until he stopped shouting and

I felt the fight go out of him. Then I realised he too had his arms around me. And so we stood together like that, at the top of that field, for what seemed like ages, not saying anything, just holding each other, while the wind kept blowing and blowing at us, tugging our clothes, and for a moment, it seemed like we were holding onto each other because that was the only way to stop us being swept away into the night. (269)

Their love might not set them free, as they hoped, but as this image suggests, it stops them being swept away, discarded and disposed of, like the rubbish blown into the barbed wire fence by the strong sea wind. It is in loving each other, caring for each other, and doing kind things for each other, the image suggests, that we are something more than refuse, "zipped up bags of organs," in the critic Patricia Waugh's words – that we are, in other words, human. The myth of the deferral is, in some modulated sense, real.

In the end, though, death comes. The image of Kathy and Tommy holding onto one another as the storm rages around them is echoed a little later, when Tommy tells Kathy that he doesn't want her to be his carer any more. He says:

I keep thinking about this river somewhere, with the water moving really fast. And these two people in the water, trying to hold onto each other, holding on as

> *hard as they can, but in the end it's just too much. The current's too strong. They've got to let go, drift apart. That's how I think it is with us. It's a shame, Kath, because we've loved each other all our lives. But in the end, we can't stay together forever.* (277)

This is the prison that Ishiguro is writing about: our powerlessness against death. "I suppose, ultimately," he has said, "I wanted to write a book about how people accept that we are mortal and we can't get away from this, and that after a certain point we are all going to die, we won't live for ever."

If Ishiguro wants to remind us of our inevitable end, it's because he wants to encourage us to make the most of things while we can – to do what we need to do to not be trash and to ease the burden of those around us. In the end, says Wai-chew Sim, the novel "becomes a story about... what we need to do before we die". It becomes a novel about seizing the day, about making your life count before it's too late. "What I was trying to get at," Ishiguro said in his *NPR Radio* interview, is that "we will all fade away and die, but people can find the energy to create little pockets of happiness and decency while we're here."

It is precisely the coupling of their everydayness with their strangeness that both makes the clones normal like us, and makes us strange like them. The clones are unable to look at their situation from an outside perspective, and so they passively accept their fate; but perhaps, through reading the novel, we can catch a glimpse of what our situation might look like were we able to stand outside it and look in.

For Ishiguro, this makes *Never Let Me Go* an optimistic novel. "This is a rather cheerful tale," he said in an interview, "the book really stresses the positive side of human nature. Humans are capable of caring deeply for one another." "Although it's a story about mortality," he has said elsewhere, "I wanted it to be a quite positive story. By having this rather negative, bleak scenario, I thought it might highlight what is actually quite positive and valuable about being alive."

Readers will have to make up their own minds about whether *Never Let Me Go* is a positive novel or not. But in the interests of balance, here are quotations from two of the most perceptive reviews, which might provide a counter to Ishiguro's point of view. Here is James Wood:

> The cloned children are being educated at school for lives of perfect pointlessness, pointless because they will die before they can grasp their adulthood. Everything they do is dipped in futility, because the great pool of death awaits them. They possess individuality, and seem to enjoy it (they fall in love, they have sex, they read George Eliot), but that individuality is a mirage, a parody of liberty. Their lives have been written in

Menand's, Louis, 'Something About Kathy' in *The New Yorker* (2005)
Tait, Theo, 'A Sinister Harvest' in *The Telegraph* (2015)
Wood, James, 'Kazuo Ishiguro's Never Let Me Go' in *The Fun Stuff* (Random House, 2013)
Wood, James, 'The Uses of Oblivion' in *The New Yorker* (2015)

Secondary

Arendt, Hannah, *Eichmann in Jerusalem: A Report on the Banality of Evil* (Penguin, 2011)
Bergsen, Henri Louis, *Laughter: An Essay on the Meaning of the Comic* (Arc Manor, 2008)
Cooper, Lydia R., 'Novelist Practice and Ethical Philosophy in Kazuo Ishiguro's *The Remains of the Day* in Groes, Sebastian and Lewis, Barry ed. *Kazuo Ishiguro: New Critical Visions of the Novels* (Palgrave Macmillan, 2011)
Currie, Mark, 'Controlling Time: Kazuo Ishiguro's *Never Let Me Go'* in Matthews, Sean and Groes, Sebastian ed. *Kazuo Ishiguro: Contemporary Critical Perspectives*
Freud, Sigmund, 'The Uncanny' in *The Uncanny* (Penguin, 2003)
Groes, Sebastian 'Something of a Lost Corner: The Representation of East Anglia in Kazuo Ishiguro's *Never Let Me Go*' in Matthews, Sean and Groes, Sebastian ed. *Kazuo Ishiguro: Contemporary*

Critical Perspectives

Groes, Sebastian and Lewis, Barry ed. *Kazuo Ishiguro: New Critical Visions of the Novels* (Palgrave Macmillan, 2011)
Jentsch, Ernst, 'On the Psychology of the Uncanny' (1906)
Lewis, Barry, *Kazuo Ishiguro* (Manchester University Press, 2000)
Lewis, Wyndham, *The Wild Body: A Soldier of Humour and Other Stories* (Penguin Classics, 2004)
Lodge, David, 'The Unreliable Narrator: Kazuo Ishiguro' in *The Art of Fiction* (Vintage, 2011)
Matthews, Sean and Groes, Sebastian ed. *Kazuo Ishiguro: Contemporary Critical Perspectives*

Mullan, John, 'On First Reading *Never Let Me Go*' in Matthews, Sean and Groes, Sebastian ed. *Kazuo Ishiguro: Contemporary Critical Perspectives*

Royle, Nicholas, *The Uncanny* (Manchester University Press, 2003)

Sage, Victor, 'The Pedagogics of Liminality: Rites of Passage in the Works of Kazuo Ishiguro' in Groes, Sebastian and Lewis, Barry ed. *Kazuo Ishiguro: New Critical Visions of the Novels* (Palgrave Macmillan, 2011)

Sim, Wai-che *Kazuo Ishiguro: A Routledge Guide* (Routledge, 2009)

Waugh, Patricia, 'Kazuo Ishiguro's Not Too Late Modernism' in Groes, Sebastian and Lewis, Barry ed. *Kazuo Ishiguro: New Critical Visions of the Novels* (Palgrave Macmillan, 2011)

Wong, Cynthia F., *Kazuo Ishiguro* (Northcote House, 2005)

Notes

First published in 2016 by
Connell Guides
Artist House
35 Little Russell Street
London WC1A 2HH

10 9 8 7 6 5 4 3 2 1

Picture credits:
p.19 © Everett/REX/Shutterstock
p.41 © Geraint Lewis/REX/Shurtterstock

A CIP catalogue record for this book is available from the British Library.
ISBN 978-1-911187-07-3

Design © Nathan Burton
Written by David Isaacs
Edited by Jolyon Connell

Assistant Editor and typeset by:
Paul Woodward & Holly Bruce

Printed in Great Britain

www.connellguides.com